Barack Obama

BY CHERYL MANSFIELD

The Child's World®
childsworld.com

Published by The Child's World®
1980 Lookout Drive • Mankato, MN 56003-1705
800-599-READ • www.childsworld.com

Acknowledgments
The Child's World®: Mary Swensen, Publishing Director
Red Line Editorial: Editorial direction and production
The Design Lab: Design

Photographs ©: Pete Souza/Official White House Photo,
cover, 1; Jason Reed/Reuters, 4; Everett Collection/
Shutterstock Images, 7; HO/Reuters, 8; Punahoe Schools/
AP Images, 11; Thomas Grauman/Corbis, 12; Sean Adair/
Reuters, 15; Ron Sachs/CNP/Corbis, 16; J. Scott Applewhite/
AP Images, 19; Aaron St. Clair/Splash News/Corbis, 21

ISBN 9781503808461
LCCN 2015958441

Printed in the United States of America
Mankato, MN
June, 2016
PA02303

ABOUT THE AUTHOR

Cheryl Mansfield was meant to write for kids. At age nine, she wrote her first nonfiction story. It was about lions. Everyone in her class read it.

Table of Contents

Obama spoke with some voters over the phone on November 4, 2008.

CHAPTER ONE

Victory

November 4, 2008, was a big night. The United States would choose a new president. Barack Obama was the Democratic **candidate.** If he won, he would become America's first African American president.

The day started as a normal day for the Obama family. Obama spoke with people. He told them why they should vote for him. His children went to school. The family had dinner at their home in Chicago. Then, they went to a hotel. They watched the **election** results. Friends and family joined them. They were excited.

Obama hoped he would win. Some people were not sure he could. He was young. He had not been in **politics** very long. And so far only white men had been president. But he had hope.

The news reported the results in each state. Excitement grew. Obama won some states. The Republican candidate, John McCain, won others. At 11:00 p.m., the winner was declared. Barack Obama had won. Everyone in the hotel room got very quiet. They had hoped for this. They had all worked very hard.

It was not quiet in nearby Grant Park. There were over 200,000 people in the park. They cheered and yelled. They supported Obama. Some had come to the park early. They wanted the best spot to see the stage. Soon, Obama would speak.

Obama and his family waved to voters after winning the presidential election.

Obama walked onto the stage with his family.
The crowd went wild. History had been made.
Barack Obama was America's 44th president. And he
was the nation's first African American president.

Barry (right) spent his childhood in Hawaii and Indonesia.

CHAPTER TWO

Childhood

Barack Hussein Obama was born in Honolulu, Hawaii. He was named for his father Barack Sr. But his parents called him Barry. His father was a black man from Kenya, Africa. Barry's mother was white. Her name was Stanley Ann Dunham. Everyone called her Ann. Barry's parents met in college. They got married. But Barack Sr. left his wife and son before Barry's first birthday. Barry's parents **divorced** when he was two. He did not see his father much after that.

When Barry was six, his mom remarried. Her husband was from Indonesia. The family moved there. Life was very different. Most roads were not paved. There were few cars. The family had a pet monkey named Tata. Barry thought it was fun to live there. His mom did not agree. She wanted him to remember he was an American. She woke early every morning. She gave him English lessons. She taught him about famous African Americans. She worried about his education. She wanted him to go to school in America. So she sent him back to Hawaii. He was ten. He lived there with his grandparents.

Barry did not fit in at his new school. Few African Americans lived in Hawaii then. But he became good at making friends. He did well in school. He liked to go to the beach. He learned to play basketball. He often played on the school courts.

Barry played basketball in high school.

Obama attended Occidental College from 1979–1981.

CHAPTER THREE

Finding His Roots

At first, Obama did not want to go to college. His mother talked him into going. He got a full **scholarship**. He went to Occidental College in California. He learned about politics. He liked to give speeches. After two years, he moved to New York City. He went to Columbia University. He moved to Chicago when he graduated. He got a job. He helped Chicago's poor people. Many were African Americans.

Obama wanted to do more. He needed a law degree. But he also wondered about his **roots**. So he went to Africa. He visited his father's family. He learned some of their language. This gave him a better understanding of his father and of himself. He was ready to attend Harvard Law School.

During law school, he returned to Chicago. He worked at a law firm. There, he met Michelle Robinson. She was his mentor. Obama wanted to date her. But she did not think it was a good idea since they worked together. Then, she changed her mind. They started dating. They married in 1992.

Obama taught classes at a Chicago university. He also worked at a law firm. But he wanted to help more people. In 1995, he ran for the Illinois State Senate. He won the seat.

In 2002, Congress was deciding whether to start a war in Iraq. **Terrorists** had attacked America. People hoped war would stop terrorists. Many people were for the war. Obama stood out. He was against it.

A terrorist attack on September 11, 2001, caused national security concerns that led to the Iraq War.

Obama wanted to become a U.S. senator. He worked on his public speaking skills. He liked how African American ministers spoke. Their voices had a lot of power. Obama studied them. He started his campaign. He spoke against the war.

Obama's popularity grew after his big 2004 speech.

CHAPTER FOUR

Making a Name

Soon, people liked Obama's speeches. He became popular. Many people knew who he was. He spoke at the Democratic National Convention in 2004. He was the main speaker. Afterward, huge crowds came to hear him speak wherever he went. He won the U.S. Senate seat by a historic amount.

By 2007, America's **economy** was in trouble. People needed jobs. America was at war. Obama wanted to help. He ran for president.

Obama grew more popular. He said he would cut **taxes** for the poor. He would end the war.

Americans voted on November 4, 2008. Obama became president on January 20, 2009.

He went to work. He signed a law to help America's economy. The law spent $800 billion. But some people became unhappy with him. The economy was slow to get better. Many people still needed jobs. Some were unhappy about changes Obama wanted to make.

Health care change was a hot topic. Most Americans had health **insurance**. But some could not afford it. Obama wanted to make it more affordable. Democrats and Republicans argued. Republicans did not want change. Democrats wanted change. But they did not agree on what the changes should be. Obama worked hard. He let Congress help shape the changes. Finally, Congress passed a bill. It was called

Obama signed the Affordable Care Act in 2010.

the Affordable Care Act. Obama signed the law
in 2010.

Obama also worked to end the Iraq War. He
pulled most American troops from Iraq in 2011. Only
150 troops remained.

By 2011, more people had jobs. America was
doing better. Obama ran for reelection. He won on
November 6, 2012.

Obama wanted more gun control. On December 14, 2012, a man shot people in Connecticut. Other shootings happened during Obama's presidency. He asked for better background checks when people bought guns. But Congress denied the bill.

Obama also worked to improve **immigration**. In 2014, he made changes to immigration laws. The changes happened gradually. Some people come to America without permission. The changes made it easier for them to stay. It also made them pay taxes. This helped the government.

Obama faced challenges. But he left his mark as the first African American president of the United States of America.

People made a memorial for those who had died in a Connecticut shooting.

TIMELINE

1960

← **August 4, 1961** Barack Obama is born in Honolulu, Hawaii.

← **1967** Obama moves to Indonesia with his mother and stepfather.

← **1971** Obama returns to Hawaii to live with his grandparents. He starts fifth grade at Punahou Academy.

← **1983** Obama graduates from Columbia University.

← **1985** Obama moves to Chicago and becomes the director of Developing Communities.

← **1987** Obama travels to Kenya to visit his father's family.

← **1988** Obama begins Harvard Law School.

← **1991** Obama graduates from Harvard Law School.

← **October 18, 1992** Obama marries Michelle Robinson.

← **1993** Obama begins working as a lawyer. He also teaches at the University of Chicago.

← **1996** Voters elect Obama into the Illinois State Senate.

← **July 4, 2004** Obama gives the keynote address at the 2004 Democratic National Convention.

← **November 4, 2008** Voters elect Obama as the 44th president of the United States.

← **November 6, 2012** Obama wins a second term as president of the United States.

2020

candidate (KAN-duh-date) A candidate is someone who runs in an election. Obama was a candidate for president of the United States.

divorced (di-VORSD) When a couple gets divorced they legally end their marriage. Obama's parents divorced when he was two.

economy (e-KON-uh-me) An economy is the money system of a country. Some people lose their jobs when the economy is bad.

election (i-LEK-shun) An election is when people choose a leader by voting. A presidential election is held every four years.

immigration (im-uh-GRAY-shun) Immigration happens when someone enters a new country to live there. Obama wanted to improve immigration.

insurance (in-SHUR-uns) Insurance is bought from a company that will pay for health care or property damage. Obama wanted to make health insurance more affordable.

politics (POL-uh-tiks) Politics are activities to gain or hold onto power in government. Obama studied politics in college.

roots (ROOTS) Roots are the people and places where someone came from. Obama wanted to learn about his roots.

scholarship (SCAH-lor-ship) A scholarship is money that a school gives to a student. Obama received a scholarship to attend college.

taxes (TAKS-is) Taxes are money that people and companies pay to the government. Obama wanted to lower taxes for poor people.

terrorists (TER-ur-ists) Terrorists are people who scare others into obedience by using violence. Terrorists attacked the United States in 2001.

In the Library

Gilpin, Caroline Crosson. *Barack Obama*. Washington, DC: National Geographic, 2014.

Kawa, Katie. *Barack Obama: First African American President*. New York: PowerKids Press, 2013.

Mattern, Joanne. *Barack Obama*. New York: Children's Press, 2013.

On the Web

Visit our Web site for links about Barack Obama: **childsworld.com/links**

Note to Parents, Teachers, and Librarians: We routinely verify our Web links to make sure they are safe and active sites. So encourage your readers to check them out!

INDEX